Go Set a Watchman by Harper Lee

Summary and Analysis

IMPORTANT

PLEASE NOTE: This is an unofficial summary and analysis of the book *Go Set a Watchman: A Novel*, by *Harper Lee* and NOT the original book.

Disclaimer

Effort has been made to ensure that the information in this book is accurate and complete. However, the author and the publisher do not warrant the accuracy of the information, text and graphics contained within the book due to the rapidly changing nature of science, research, known and unknown facts. The author and the publisher do not hold any responsibility for errors, omissions or contrary interpretation of the subject matter herein. This book is presented solely for motivational and informational purposes only.

All Rights Reserved.

No part of this publication or the information in it may be quoted from or reproduced in any form by means such as printing, scanning, photocopying or otherwise without prior written permission of the copyright holder.

Table of Contents

Introduction 7

Summary of Part I 10
    Chapter 1 11
    Chapter 2 14
    Chapter 3 16

Summary of Part II 19
    Chapter 4 20
    Chapter 5 22

Summary of Part III 25
    Chapter 6 26
    Chapter 7 27
    Chapter 8 29
    Chapter 9 31
    Chapter 10 33

Summary of Part IV 34
    Chapter 11 35
    Chapter 12 38

Summary of Part V 40
    Chapter 13 41
    Chapter 14 44

Summary of Part VI 46
    Chapter 15 47
    Chapter 16 52
    Chapter 17 54

Summary of Part VII 56
    Chapter 18 57
    Chapter 19 63

Analysis 65
    List of important characters 65
    Structure and Style 67
    Context and Theme/Motif 68
    Symbolisms 70
    Plot Arguments 77
    Publication Controversy 81

Review Conclusion 82

Introduction

In 1960, Harper Lee's debut novel To Kill a Mockingbird was published. It went on to win the 1961 Pulitzer Prize for Fiction and received numerous awards. Since then, readers have been clamoring for an update or sequel to the book that brought us the Finches of Maycomb, Alabama in the 1930s.

Now, after more than fifty years later, that wish is fulfilled. **Go Set a Watchman** was published last July 14, 2015. Jean Louise "Scout" Finch, the protagonist in the story, is now twenty-six years old. This sequel book tells about her trip home, the changes she sees, and the things she discovers about her world and her family against the backdrop of the South in the 1950s. The book aims to add new meaning, depth, and context to the classic that is To Kill a Mockingbird.

Go Set a Watchman is chronologically set twenty years after the events of To Kill a Mockingbird. However, various reports states that this book is actually the first draft of TKAM; and under Lee's editor, it was heavily revised and polished until it was published as To Kill A Mockingbird in 1960.

It is common knowledge that Harper Lee was against the idea of publishing a sequel for the past fifty or so years. This caused a little controversy when the drafts of the supposed sequel, along with how in control Harper Lee is of her work, were discovered. However, despite the circumstances surrounding the book's publication today, it is best to view it as an essential companion to the first book and as a new lens with which we can view our own society.

Go Set a Watchman is published by HarperCollins, the company that acquired J.B. Lippincott the original publisher of To Kill a Mockingbird. In its first week of being published, about 700,000+ copies have been sold all over the world. As of August 11, 2015, the book has been rated 27,610 times on Goodreads.com with an average rating of 3.52 stars.

The book is available in hardcover and eBook formats at Amazon, Barnes & Noble, Nook, iBooks, other online sites and offline bookstores.

The author, Harper Lee, is now retired and is residing in an assisted-living facility in Alabama, United States.

Summary of Part I

Chapter 1

The first chapter of *Go Set a Watchman* starts with Jean Louise "Scout" Finch returning to Maycomb, Alabama. On this annual home trip, Jean Louise elected to travel by train instead of a plane. The train ride also allowed Scout to marvel at the different changes in the country, most notably with the television antennas on Negro houses. The author also describes the origin of Maycomb County, and relates the story of Cousin Joshua that made Jean Louise laugh at the memory.

She is greeted by Henry "Hank" Clinton on the Maycomb Junction train station. At this point in the story, it is revealed that her father, Atticus Finch, who is now seventy-two years old, has rheumatoid arthritis and hence can't pick her up from the station. Hank's story is also told with descriptions by Jean Louise as the one who had the right to kiss her, and as someone who is the same "kind" of Jean Louise. The first few pages also tell the readers that Jem has died a few years ago. It was a described as a nightmare.

On their drive home, Henry and Jean Louise began talking about how each other have been. It is revealed that Henry came into picture a few years after To Kill a Mockingbird ended. Henry boarded at Miss Stephanie's home.

He was raised by a single mother who eventually died and he was left to his own devices. After high school, he went to war and came home with six false teeth -- and a scar under his right eye, extending to under his nose. It is unclear how Henry got them because he does not like to talk about it at all. Upon returning to Maycomb, Henry went to University and studied law. He fell in love with Jean Louise despite her tomboyish ways.

Henry wastes no time on proposing to Jean Louise (albeit offhandedly at first). Jean Louise answers 'not yet'. She says she wants to be like Dr. Schweitzer and keep on playing until she is thirty. This turned into the beginning of an argument, prompting Jean Louise to really think about marrying Henry. She thinks she was almost in love with him.

That's the thing, Jean Louise thought, love should be unequivocal (you are or you are not). She does not want Henry to be her easy way out. She would rather pursue the path to spinsterhood at the present than be miserable about it in the future.

The two were friends again by the end of the chapter when Jean Louise apologized and asked Henry for advice on how to be an enchantress to men.

Chapter 2

Jean Louise and Hank arrives home and was greeted by Atticus and Aunt Alexandra. After the usual questions on regarding their health, she pesters her father and aunt to tell her news about Maycomb. She says that all she reads are in between the lines of the Maycomb Tribune and that no one ever writes to her anything.

Aunt Alexandra tells her of Cousin Edgar's son's death and the Merriweathers' divorce. Aunt Xandra also comments on Jean Louise' choice of outfit and the supposed impression she is getting from her other relatives and the people of Maycomb. This irked Jean Louise, forcing her into a tirade about how she has always dressed the way she wants and it has nothing to do with her being from New York.

This would have turned into a worse argument between the aunt and niece if Atticus did not intervene. He asked Jean Louise to apologize to her aunt and to Hank. Despite her apology, Aunt

Alexandra was still visibly disapproving of Jean Louise's uninhibited ways.

Jean Louise paid no attention to this and focused on how Atticus has been spending his days lately. She asked him if he was available to play the next day but Atticus declined citing that he had a meeting. The two agreed to play golf on Monday afternoon instead. Atticus also asks Jean Louise what kind of news from the South has been reported in New York papers.

Jean Louise told him that state news only gets to the papers when the Governor's indiscrete dealings hit tabloids. As for political news, she said, the papers does not care much and she herself has only been paying attention to the bus strikes, the lack of conviction for the Mississippi case, and the NAACP Christmas seals she received last year.

Hank and Jean Louise made arrangements to meet back later that night before Hank left to go back to the office; Atticus went with him.

Chapter 3

This chapter begins with a description about Aunt Alexandra's life, and how their relationship has always been made of uneasy cordiality ever since she agreed to live with them. Jean Louise describes her aunt as an incurable gossip, had boarding school manners, and had no self-doubt in her vocabulary. Aunt Alexandra is separated from her husband of thirty-three years and had one son, Francis, who now lived in Birmingham.

The narrative proceeds to describe Aunt Alexandra's and Jean Louise's last skirmish two years ago. It was after Jem's funeral. Aunt Alexandra told Jean Louise that her father needs her and that it's time for her to come home for good. Jean Louise bristled at the thought. She knows that her father would tell her if he needs her. But Aunt Alexandra doesn't see this, she always hasn't. That is why they've always had arguments. In Aunt Alexandra's mind, the decision for Jean Louise to come home to Maycomb was already decided.

Jean Louise tells her aunt that she will not say home and if she did Atticus will be very sad. She tries to tell her aunt that her father understands perfectly and that he would not want Jean Louise home either. Then Aunt Alexandra's retort on how her dead brother, Jem, has always worried about Jean Louise's thoughtlessness.

This unnerves Jean Louise; she tells herself that Jem does not think like that. Still, she returned to New York and had stopped worrying about how thoughtless she was. Aunt Alexandra went to live with Atticus when he was diagnosed with arthritis, making Jean Louise grateful for her aunt.

Now, two years later, Alexandra tells Jean Louise that she is giving a Coffee for her return. Jean Louise replied that such event is horrifying enough but would love one. Coffees were Maycombian tradition where girls who come home are re-introduced to other girls of their own age who have remained in Maycomb.

Jean Louise asked her aunt about how Hank was doing and how she would think of considering him as her aunt's future nephew. Aunt Alexandra argues that dating Hank is a lot different from marrying him. Her aunt went on to a tirade about how Hank and his family had no background and were just white redneck trash. This just made Jean Louise reel inside. So Jean Louise cordially told her aunt to 'go pee in her hat'.

Summary of Part II

Chapter 4

The second part of the novel begins with descriptions of Maycomb, Alabama, how the town came to be, the different families living in it, and how it has changed after the Second World War and after Jean Louise left.

Henry and Jean Louise were at the Maycomb Hotel dining room. Jean Louise tells Henry how she is a conservatively resistant to change and that the only thing she likes is how the smell of the place is gone. She remembers a game Hot-Grease-In-The-Kitchen, some snatches of childhood memory, all of which she couldn't quite pin down. This all left her with an odd feeling that time had passed her by.

The couple's talk centered on Jean Louise' worry on marrying the wrong kind of person for her. She talks about how after the first few years of marriage, men would have affairs, couples would fight, and the cycle goes on as what she has learned from watching Madison Avenue young married couples. To this,

Henry just stares at her and tells her how he has never heard her so cynical. Their talk is interrupted by the waiter carrying the check and with Jean Louise looking forward to her visit with Uncle Jack.

Chapter 5

Henry and Jean Louise left the hotel in Henry's automobile. Henry asked Jean Louise if she remembers Jem falling out of their old square Buick on their way to Barker's Eddy for a swim and she laughed at the memory. He also tells Jean Louise that a planing mill was constructed on the eddy and swimming is now prohibited. On the drive, Henry was remembering his Law School days, young Jean Louise, Jem, and of course, Dill.

Jean Louise tells him that Dill was in Italy. After the war, Dill has stayed in Europe. Jean Louise also fitfully remembers back all the summers with Jem and Dill, the games they played, the make-believe plays they've come up with. The chapter narrates how on one summer, the three young kids came up their own revival right at Dill's aunt's (Miss Rachel) yard by the fish pool.

A revival is a church event where every summer, the different churches in Maycomb holds a renowned minister to speak to the entire congregation of different churches. But sometimes when the three churches disagree on the speaker, the honoraria, or other terms, each church holds their own revivals instead.

In the three kids' own revival, Jem portrayed Reverend Moorehead (who was the speaker for their own church' revival), Dill dressed up as the Holy Ghost among other mini tasks, and Scout was the to-be-baptized churchgoer. Just when they were baptizing (dunking) a naked Scout in the fish pool, Aunt Rachel arrived, angry at the bed sheet-costumed Dill, hit him with a stick and hauled him back home.

Meanwhile, Jem and Scout saw their father and a couple who turned out to be Reverend Moorehead himself and his wife, standing by their front door. The couple was at their home for dinner and had witnessed the kids' play. During dinner and after Reverend Moore said prayers for the forgiveness of the children's actions, Atticus excused himself. Jean Louise worried that she has disappointed her father.

Calpurnia, their cook, whispered to Jean Louise that Atticus was only out in the yard, laughing.

Present time, Henry and Jean Louise have reached Finch's Landing. It was a piece of land by the river and was first owned by Atticus Finch's great-great-grandfather. Henry tells Jean Louise that the land has been sold. This surprises Jean Louise, she hates surprises and changes.

Jean Louise then opens up to Henry about her aunt's disapproval of him. To this, Henry responds that he has known all his life. He opens up to Jean Louise that he can now support them both, start a family, and even run in the state legislature. Their talk ended into a dare with the two of them jumping into the water fully clothed.

Summary of Part III

Chapter 6

The next morning, Jean Louise was woken up by Aunt Alexandra. It turns out that the whole Maycomb has been filled in (courtesy of Mary Webster) of Jean Louise and Henry's apparent skinny-dipping escapade at Finch's Landing the previous night. Jean Louise took this in stride, and even joked about it with her father. Aunt Alexandra did not find it funny at all.

Since it was a Sunday, the family went to church where they met with Uncle Jack. Dr. John Hale Finch was Atticus and Alexandra's younger brother and specialized in orthopedics. But this passion lies in Victorian literature earning him the title of becoming Maycomb County's most learned licensed eccentric. Uncle Finch greeted her with a remark on her and Henry 'mollocking around' in the river, just nineteen hours after her arrival. How fast gossip flies in small towns! Jean Louise tells her uncle that she will visit him in the afternoon and marched off into the church for Sunday school which she barely listened to.

Chapter 7

The Sunday service has began and Jean Louise is left watching and making observations about the similarities of Atticus, Uncle Jack and Aunt Alexandra. They were siblings after all. These meditations were interrupted by Henry who winked at her when the collection plate passed by her pew. Aunt Alexandra saw this and her face was murderous. Suddenly, the whole congregation was surprised when Mrs. Haskins (the organist) played the Doxology differently. It was the first time that this has happened, in Jean Louise's recollection. The congregation followed the new song interpretation without question for the rest of the service.

While Jean Louise was thinking of who was responsible of the change, her thoughts veered to their church's new minister, Mr. Stone.

But remembering that he was tone deaf, Jean Louise tried to pay attention to the minister's text taken from Chapter 21 Verse 6 of Isaiah:

"For thus hath the Lord said unto me,
Go, set a watchman, let him declare what he seeth."

When the service ended, Jean Louise saw Dr. Finch corner Herbert Jemson, the Maycomb Methodist Church's music director. Dr. Finch was already complaining about the new songs and their renditions. It was revealed that Jemson was sent to a music camp at Camp Charles Wesley and was told to sing the songs differently compared to how the congregation used to. Dr. Finch argued that the music instructor at that camp were snobs, pointing out that only Englishman songs were removed from their previous song lists but these same instructors wanted them to sing the Doxology like they were all in the Westminster Abbey. Jemson countered that he was only testing the waters; he likes the old ones better.

Chapter 8

Henry and Atticus left for a meeting that Sunday afternoon. Jean Louise was clearing her father's papers when she found a pamphlet, The Black Plague, arguing white people's supremacy over Negroes. She asked Aunt Alexandra where it came from and was told it was her father's. Further probing led Aunt Alexandra telling Jean Louise that Atticus and Henry were part of Maycomb's Citizens' Council and that they are meeting at that moment in the town courthouse.

Jean Louise walked out of the house and straight to town, willing to find out what Atticus and Henry were really up to.

She walked up to the Colored balcony section of the courthouse, below she saw Atticus, Henry, William Willoughby, and other respectable men in Alabama. She stayed in her inconspicuous place while listening to Mr. Grady O'Hanlon talking about they should uphold the Southern way of life, and how no niggers and no Supreme Court can stop them. Jean Louise barely heard Mr. O'Hanlon's racist speech; her mind was off to watching Atticus defend a black man accused of rape.

Jean Louise walked out of the courthouse in a daze, heaving, feeling sick. Unconsciously, she walked back to her old neighborhood, thinking about their former neighbors and friends. She stopped at her home that was now an ice cream parlor.

Jean Louise bought ice cream and proceeded to the tables and chairs in the back yard. She was still heaving, feeling nauseous and dizzy to what Atticus had done.

Chapter 9

The next chapter details Atticus' life and how he started his family. It also describes how Atticus played the role of both a mother and father when his wife died and left him with two young children. He raised Jem and Scout as best as he could and despite his age, he kept up with his children without imposing on them.

Jean Louise grew up not really needing a mother except for the time when she got her first period and Atticus and Jem looked as helpless at her dilemma. It was a good thing Calpurnia, their old cook, was there to help.

The chapter proceeds to describe Jean Louise's feelings of alienation towards being a girl and could not quite comprehend her new roles. Adding to her dilemma was when Jem turned sixteen and started dating. She could not keep up with his brother anymore. Jean Louise was left to her own devices and her companions were Atticus and Dr. Finch who helped her traverse the path of adolescence. Still, Jean Louise went through the 'motions of complying with the regulations governing the behavior of teenage girls from good families'.

When Jean Louise felt alone, she felt safe with the knowledge of the love and moral force of her father who will always stand beside her. She was sent to college and Atticus even encouraged her to try out her life in New York. Atticus wanted her daughter to be able to fend for herself when he gets old.

Jean Louise realizes that most, if not all, her decisions were based upon Atticus' personal credo and morals. She realizes that she did not even know how much she worshipped Atticus.

Chapter 10

Jean Louise was still at the ice cream parlor when she vomited her entire Sunday dinner by the fence that separated Miss Rachel's garden from the Finch back yard. She thought of Dill. But he was gone. Her nausea returned, her ice cream had melted, and the ice cream man returned to clean up the melting ice cream pool. She guessed the man to be one of the Cunningham's but did not know his name.

Jean Louise returned home still sick. She phone Uncle Jack and told him that they'll meet the next day. She told Aunt Alexandra that she's sick and to tell Henry she is indisposed when he comes at night.

Jean Louise is hurt like hell too but she does not tell Aunt Alexandra that. Instead, she goes to bed and fell asleep. If only Jean Louise had insight, she could have discovered the barriers of her highly selective and insular world. She would have noticed that she has lived a life with a defect. Jean Louise was born color blind.

Summary of Part IV

Chapter 11

The chapter is another flashback when Jean Louise was in sixth grade. At about the time when she got her first period and stopped playing with the boys during recess, Scout learns from an older classmate named Ada Belle about another classmate who got pregnant. It was rumored that the classmate's daddy was the father.

This confused Scout and she asked the other girls what 'pregnant' was. The girls explained that after a girl gets her period, she could get pregnant when a boy hugs her, kisses her, and ... But Scout could only think of how her classmate, Albert Cunningham, the one who she helped in some tests, kissed her and stuck out his tongue at her. She was pregnant.

Scout cut class and went home. She could not tell Atticus, Jem, even Calpurnia, for fear of the disgrace that she has brought to their family. She gradually became withdrawn. Her very limited readings about pregnancy and birth told her that she got nine months before the baby arrives, on October.

That is why right after school on the thirtieth of September, Scout walked to the town water tank tower. While she was contemplating the way she should jump and who would cry on her funeral, someone grabbed her arms from behind and led her down the tower. It was Henry. He was crying, asking Scout what was wrong with her. Scout was trembling, not uttering a word so Henry did not pester her and brought her home.

They were met by Calpurnia. Henry had to go back to his job at the Jitney Jungle so Cal and Scout were left alone. Calpurnia urged Scout to tell her what was wrong, promising she would not tell Atticus. Scout bawled that she was having a baby the next day and told her everything. Calpurnia was incredulous over the Old Sarum girls who filled Scout's head with ridiculous stories. She comforted the young girl, told her that she was not pregnant and informed her of the accurate information on baby-making and what couples do.

Scout was back to being delighted of her life. She dozed in the living room and was awakened by Jem who has just arrived from football practice. Scout was afraid that Calpurnia has told on her. But then she knew Cal wouldn't.

Jem was leafing through a football magazine and told Scout that if ever there was something that she might not want to tell Atticus, she should let Jem know and he will take care of it for her. Jem left the living room and left Scout dazed.

Chapter 12

Jean Louise wakes up the next day wanting the previous day to be a nightmare. She had breakfast with Aunt Alexandra and Atticus whom she could not even look in the eye. Henry arrived and brought news about Calpurnia's grandchild who was in jail for killing a person while driving drunk. Atticus was asked to defend him.

Atticus tells Henry that he will accept the case since NAACP lawyers are waiting for something for this to happen to cause trouble and Atticus does not want that to happen. Jean Louise could not continue listening to the growing conversation, she left the room.

After breakfast, Aunt Alexandra tasks Jean Louise of buying supplies in town. Mr. Fred, the Jitney Jungle owner, strikes her a curious question about not staying home this time. Jean Louise reflects that not merely Atticus and Henry were separately from but also, the whole Maycomb County was leaving her too.

And she blamed herself for it. She returned home to bring home the groceries and drive Atticus to work. She still could not look at him, listen to him or talk to him.

Jean Louise decides to visit Calpurnia's home. She was a lot older now. When Jean Louise began talking to her, she used her company manners and spoke to Jean Louise with haughtiness and detachment. Jean Louise could not understand what would make a person who raised her and Jem turn into something like that. Jean Louise drove home unsettled.

Summary of Part V

Chapter 13

Jean Louise goes back home and finds Aunt Alexandra preparing for the Coffee. She sighed heavily upon hearing the women who were invited, all women who are either younger than her or had not shared any experiences with.

She also tells her that she visited Calpurnia and her aunt was shocked. Aunt Alexandra went on to racist rant just like how Mr. O'Hanlon had. Jean Louise went out the kitchen to the living room where she pondered on how the same people who were Christian and have taught her right from wrong were not creeped out of the ideas they were spouting that everything that has been happening has been on account of the Negroes. She realizes that all these people could not have changed just like that. It was she who has changed.

The Coffee started at 10:30 and Jean Louise mentally divided her guests into groups: The Newlyweds, The Diaper Set, the Light Brigade and the Perennial

Hopefuls. All groups of women she couldn't stand and have not the slightest idea of what to say to them.

She managed to engage in a conversation with Hester Sinclair and this turned out to be dud when went on spouting off her incredibly narrow-minded beliefs. She was asked about her life in New York and thought about how different it was from Maycomb; how she has learned what human decency was when growing up in Maycomb. She just could not comprehend how she was raised by Atticus, a man who lived by truth, and taught his children never to take advantage of anyone less fortunate (not just Negroes) whether by social position, brains or wealth, and the reverse will be despised.

Still she did not see the truth of this man until now because she only looked at people's faces and never in their true hearts. Jean Louise realizes that she was stone blind and, reminded of Mr. Stone's (the minister) watchman, she thought needs a watchman. A watchman who will tell her the difference between what a man says and what a man really means. She needs a watchman who will tell everybody those twenty-six years is too long to play a joke on anybody.

Chapter 14

After the Coffee, Jean Louise goes to visit Uncle Finch and had dinner together. Jean Louise right away asks her uncle what was the matter with Atticus. Uncle Finch began to ask Jean Louise about different personalities of Maycomb's history that she has learned from her early years, about the Civil War, about how this war is incidental to what was happening now, and how it was incidental to Jean Louise's own personal war. Piece by piece she urged Jean Louise to try to piece each information together.

Jean Louise tried to follow her uncle's string of stories and runaround, but she saw through him not giving any straight answer. She tells him this and Uncle Finch just tells her that he cannot give her an answer.

Because it is neither within his power nor of his place to do so, uncle Finch urged Jean Louise to come back to him when she feels like she can't stand the things that are happening to her and calls her Childe Roland.

44

Jean Louise was dismissed and went home. She did not see Uncle Finch visibly getting worried after their talk and pick up the telephone.

Summary of Part VI

Chapter 15

Jean Louise finds herself eating ice cream at her old home that was now an ice cream shop. She sat dreamily in the back yard reconstructing her old house, populating the place with her former neighbors and remembered the time she went to her first school dance.

Traditionally, each senior invites his or her younger brother or sister to the dance. Jean Louise wasn't sure if Jem had some kind of deal with Henry to take her to the dance while Jem with her then girlfriend Irene who was from Abbottsville.

Jean Louise was self-conscious about her figure and was told off by Calpurnia that she looked the same. She bought false bosoms for her dress; and when Calpurnia saw this, suggested that they should be sewn in. A few hours before the event, Jean Louise realized she does not know how to dance.

She phoned Uncle Finch at Atticus' suggestion. Jean Louise learned simple box steps in an hour and ultimately forgot about sewing in the false bosoms she bought for her dress. They left home and Jean Louise had a great, fun time talking with other girls and boys and dancing with Hank or other boys. Even if she can't dance to every song, she wished the night would last forever. Until...

Jem danced his duty dance with Jean Louise, exchanged a few retorts only siblings can say to each other, and right after Henry took the next one. He suddenly goggled at her while dancing and led the two of them outside claiming it was getting inside the hall. He led her in front of the school building and, since it was dark out, asked Jean Louise to feel her front. Jean Louise did so and felt her right false bosom in the center of her chest and the other under her left armpit.

She cried. Henry comforted her in his gentlemanly ways, telling her that no one even noticed it. Jean Louise wanted to go home but Henry stopped her, yanked the false bosoms out and flung them as far away as he could.

The two went back to the hall and enjoyed the rest of the dance until it ended at eleven. Henry brought her back home and kissed her twice by their front door.

The next morning at school, Jean Louise was in deep thoughts of her crush Henry and was interrupted only when her homeroom teacher announced a special assembly of the junior and senior schools.

The principal, Mr. Tuffett, led the student body to the front of the school building and pointed at the school billboard which now read: IN THE SERVICE OF THEIR COUNTR. The last letter was blocked by Jean Louise's falsies. The principal wants a signed statement of the perpetrator by two o'clock that afternoon.

Jean Louise, Hank and Jem were in a dilemma during recess. Henry could not confess for fear of being expelled. Henry would not let Jean Louise confess either because he could not hold his held high if he will let his date do it either.

Henry skipped his study hall session to go to town and consult his lawyer. When he returned, he told Jean Louise to write the confession she did it and deliver it to the principal's office before noon. When Jean Louise got to the office and handed the piece of paper, the principal took it, and without reading it, threw it to the trash bin. It turns out that Henry convinced almost the entire female population of the school to submit a similar confession. Mr. Tuffett was incredulous but he couldn't do anything about it.

Jean Louise asked Henry if Atticus had anything to say to her. To this, Henry told her that everything anybody tells their lawyer's confidential and that Atticus will not say anything to her.

This jolts Jean Louise back to the present.

Chapter 16

Jean Louise finds herself in her father's office but he was at the post office. Henry was present and invited her for coffee-time at the drugstore. Noticing something was off with Jean Louise, Henry asked how her meeting with the ladies has been. Jean Louise told him about the guff Hester and her husband has been spouting off. Henry counters that Hester believes everything her husband says because she loves her man. Jean Louise tells Henry that if that's what it means to marry, to lose one's own identity, then she will never marry. Henry further asks her what's the matter and Jean Louise tells him about how she saw him and his father at the Citizens' Council and that made her sick.

Henry tried to explain by telling a story about how Atticus once joined the Klan before it went on cross-burning. That it was better to see men's real motive behind their acts. Henry further explains that men must conform to some demands to their community so they can be of service to it. He tells her that he wants to live in Maycomb, to keep the respect of the town, and make a name for himself as a lawyer.

By this point, Jean Louise has walked out of the drugstore, Henry following her, asking her to just listen to him. Jean Louise tells Henry that all she sees in Henry is a scared little man, scared to stand on his own two feet and scared of Maycomb.

When asked what she expected Henry to do in his situation, she told him to quite the Citizens' Council and be a man. Henry tells her that it is different for him and Jean Louise. She was a Finch while he was trash. If he does something out of the norm, it would mean the end of him. To him, it was not worth it.

Jean Louise retorts that she can't live with a hypocrite.

A voice spoke behind her saying why she cannot. She turned around and found her father, eyebrows raised, smiling at her.

Chapter 17

Atticus asked Henry to leave them and Jean Louise and her father went to his office. Jean Louise asks him if he has known about Henry and he said yes. He also tells her that Uncle Jack called and told him that Jean Louise is upset about something. She told him that she was upset with Atticus for joining the Citizens' Council.

The father and daughter engage in a to and fro word battle over their convictions. Atticus is firm that the Negroes are still on the infancy as a people and they are not worthy of the full civil liberties of a citizen. He says these in a calm disposition, helping Jean Louise see through his reasons, that what he is doing in the Citizens' Council is purely for defense.

Jean Louise, on the other hand, tries to be calm hearing Atticus' reasons but fails to do so. Her own loud invective bordered on how she felt betrayed from her father's ways, for she has never seen Atticus address Negroes with insolence or treated them badly. She told him that she wished he told her there was difference between justice and justice and right and right. She told him that even if she agreed with Atticus' statement regarding Negroes being backward, illiterate, and shiftless and some are no good, the two will haven't agreed on one thing. She says Atticus is denying that Negroes are human because he is denying them hope.

Jean Louise tells Atticus that he has cheated on her, and she will never forgive him. Atticus responds by saying that he had to kill Scout but that he loves her. She tells him not to dare say that and that she'll never believe anything he says and will despise everything he stood for.

As Jean Louise grew angrier, she cursed more. Atticus just stayed calm, never raising his voice, but further taunts Jean Louise to stop it, his general call to order back when she still believed in him. Wordlessly, she prayed for God to take her away.

Summary of Part VII

Chapter 18

Jean Louise did not know how she managed to get home but she did and she started to pack right away. Aunt Alexandra came to her room, asking what she was doing, and eventually figured out that she and Atticus has a fight after Jean Louise' snappy retorts.

When her aunt tells her that no Finch runs, Jean Louise turned her angry outburst towards her aunt. She stopped when she noticed Aunt Alexandra crying which she never saw before. She apologized to her and told her that she is never coming to Maycomb and wouldn't ever want to see anyone from Maycomb either.

As Jean Louise was leaving, Dr. Finch arrived asking her where she's going. She tells her that she's off to Maycomb Junction and will sit there until the first train arrives and she's off. Just after she deposited her suitcase on the trunk, Dr. Finch surprised her with a backhand swipe to right of her face and another one to her left. She stumbled, her world spinning, tasting blood on her mouth. Dr. Finch said he was trying to get attention.

Dr. Finch gave her a handkerchief and led her back inside the house. He also gave her a glass of whiskey and told to sit and stay quiet. Her uncle excused herself to the kitchen where he got a drink for himself, trying to calm his nerves for striking a woman, something he has never done in his life. Jean Louise was exhausted and was getting high from the alcohol.

Her uncle returned and Jean Louise tells him she knows that he knows about everything that happened that afternoon. Dr. Finch confirmed it, he followed her to town, and he earlier phoned Aunt Alexandra to tell her about what happened during the Coffee that morning.

Jean Louise only agreed to talk to him if he would talk straight to her. Dr. Finch went on telling Jean Louise his earlier roundabout way of talking to her was only meant to soften her coming into this world, her way of becoming her own person. Dr. Finch tells her that every man's watchman is his conscience. That for so long Jean Louise' conscience was attached to Atticus, assuming that her answers will always be like Atticus' answers, she confused him with God, and she never saw him as a man with his own mistakes.

But when Jean Louise saw Atticus doing something that seemed to be against this conscience, she could not stand it. It's as if she got to kill herself, or kill him so that she could live. Dr. Finch reveals that he and Atticus have long wondered when this would happen and over what. It was then that Jean Louise realized that Atticus allowed her to argue on, not even defending himself.

He was allowing her to destroy her gods, break her icons, and reduce him to a human being. Dr. Finch also tells that it was courageous of her to stop running and face her father even if she was being a turnip-sized bigot.

Jean Louise, confused at this, pulled out a dictionary and read the word's definition to her uncle. Dr. Finch further elaborates that when a bigot meets someone who challenges his beliefs; he stays rigid and doesn't even listen. Blindly striking and lashing out, not giving anybody elbow room in their minds for their ideas.

Dr. Finch tells Jean Louise that his father has his beliefs and more importantly, he lives by the law. He says Atticus will be the first to stop somebody beating someone up, just like what Jean Louise did. He continues to tell her that Jean Louise is color blind, she only see people and still unable to think racially.

This seemed to have tired her uncle and asked her to drive her home and to also fetch her father. Jean Louise was reluctant at first, but Dr. Finch urged her on to meet her father, the one whom she have never met and be in for a surprise. He also risked urging Jean Louise to think about coming home. He says that Maycomb, the South needs her; that she'd be surprised there'd be people a lot of people on her side.

Still, Jean Louise counters that she does not want to live in a place that doesn't agree with her. Her uncle tells her that it takes some kind of maturity to live in the South these days and she was showing the beginnings of it.

Then Jean Louise asks her uncle what she's going to do with Henry. He tells her that to let him down easy because he is not her kind and that this has nothing to do with being trash.

Jean Louise also asks why Dr. Finch took so much trouble for Jean Louise that day. He tells her that she and Jem were his dream children, gave him something long ago and that he was trying to pay his debts. To Jean Louise' surprise, Dr. Finch revealed that he fell in love with her mother years ago. Dr. Finch was equally surprised that Atticus and Aunt Alexandra have never even told her.

Jean Louise tells her uncle that she felt ashamed of herself, all the yelling around and the things she didn't even know. Dr. Finch assured her that she should not worry herself and that she should go get her father. She left him after he recited a poem, and only when she was halfway to town that she remembered the last lines and shouted it back to her uncle in the distance.

Chapter 19

Jean Louise walked into the foyer of her father's office. She saw Henry and planned for their leave-taking at seven-thirty that night. She was now useless to Henry other than being his oldest friend.

She was startled by her father's voice as he he asked if she was ready, while walking out of his office. Jean Louise can't believe that he can say that to her after she tried to obliterate him. She tried to apologize to her father; but Atticus tells her that he is proud of her. When she looked up to him, he was beaming at her, and told her that he hoped for a daughter who will hold ground for her beliefs and even stand up to her own father.

When her father asked, she tells him that she learned the ring-tailed variety of cussing right in Maycomb. And with the things she learned, she wants to crush the man who's trying to preserve her world; she wants to stamp out all people like him. She realizes that it will be a matter of balance, like flying an airplane.

Jean Louise realizes she can't beat him but can't join either.

Jean Louise tells Atticus that she thinks she loves him very much. She saw her old enemy relax and they went home. Jean Louise thought that somebody, maybe Jem, walked over her grave. She got inside the car, careful not to bump her head.

Analysis

List of important characters

Jean Louise "Scout" Finch – the twenty-six-year-old protagonist of the story, Atticus Finch's daughter

Atticus Finch – father of Jean Louise and Jem; a lawyer and one of the most respected men in Maycomb

Henry "Hank" Clinton – a lawyer working under Atticus Finch; his character was not included in To Kill a Mockingbird

Dr. John Hale "Uncle Jack" Finch – Atticus and Alexandra's younger brother; also a retired orthopedic surgeon

Alexandra "Aunt Alexandra" Finch Hancock – Atticus' sister, separated from his husband. She stays with Atticus and helps keep house.

Jeremy "Jem" Finch – Atticus' son and Jean Louise' older brother

Charles "Dill" Baker Harris – Jem and Scout's childhood friend whom Jean Louise has not heard anything from in years

Calpurnia – the Finches' former black cook and housekeeper.

Structure and Style

Go Set a Watchman is divided into seven parts and nineteen chapters. Being a sequel to To Kill a Mockingbird, it contained many repeated descriptions of places and events that occurred in TKAM.

One of the main differences between the two works is that GSAW is written in limited third person point of view. This allows the readers to get an almost omniscient view of the things that occur in the story. This is also effective in giving the readers a glimpse of the events which occurred after the TKAM storyline ended.

The third person narrative can also be a way for the author to express the protagonist's growth. Scout, after all, is already a young adult in the story.

Context and Theme/Motif

The novel is set in the deeply racist South with the height of the Civil Rights Movement in the backdrop, particularly in Maycomb, Alabama in the 1950s. It should also be taken into account that Jean Louise, the story protagonist, has been living in New York for the past five years. At that time, New York is an entirely different place from her Southern hometown.

The story could also be viewed through the lens of young woman in the 1950s. Compared to today, society's expectations of what a woman should be and do are a lot different.

Adding all these in the mix creates a compelling theme of a person's journey through disillusionment and rediscovery of the real world. This central motif of an older Jean Louise going back to Maycomb, finding out the kind of person Atticus is and dealing with all that is comparable to a coming-of-age story.

Another recurring motif on the novel is that places and people change. Changes can occur physically like a person getting old or new houses and buildings in town. But oftentimes, people also change. We can either change with them, just watch them change, or even we can change with them.

Symbolisms

Go Set a Watchman

The book's title is the primary symbolism in the story. The phrase is first mentioned in Chapter 7 by Minister Stone as part of a liturgical text reading of Isaiah 21:6: "For thus hath the Lord said unto me,/ Go, set a watchman, let him declare what he seeth."

It was again explained by Dr. Finch on Chapter 18 when he explained to Jean Louise that for the longest time she has made her own father her watchman. And that was why she felt so upset when she found out what Atticus was doing.

Literally, it means setting another person to guard or protect yourself or others. But in the novel's case, a watchman is one's conscience, a person's moral compass. The phrase symbolizes Jean Louise's need to set her own watchman. She needs to fully form her own conscience and direct her own moral compass so that she can become her own person.

Childe Roland

Dr. Finch first uses this to address Jean Louise in Chapter 14. In the story, it is known that Dr. Finch is an appreciator of Victorian esthetes and has long taught Jean Louise about different authors from the era.

The phrase is taken from a Robert Browning poem entitled Childe Roland to the Dark Tower Came. *Roland* has references to medieval settings while *childe* is a medieval term for an untested knight. The poem goes to describe the poem's protagonist as he questions a man who tells him the directions to a dark tower. The protagonist faces different hardships, both imaginary and real, in his journey. And when he finally arrives at the tower, the poem ends. What the protagonist sees is not revealed.

Childe Roland symbolizes Jean Louise who was in her own quest back in Maycomb and as she finds out what changed so much.

Jem and his death

Everyone who has read To Kill a Mockingbird would surely be surprised to learn of Jem's death in GSAW. The character death also symbolizes a figurative departure towards what was once Jean Louise' childhood even if she does not recognize this at first.

On the last few lines on the last chapter of GSAW, Jean Louise thought that someone may have walked over her grave. She said this in reference to the stressful experience she just had, but she also thought of Jem who she thought would do such a stupid thing for her.

Charles "Dill" Baker Harris

The character of Dill was inspired by Harper Lee's real life friend, Truman Capote. In the story, Dill never returned to Maycomb after the war and even only found out about Jem's death on his own. Dill was a prominent figure in Jem and Scout's lives as they were growing up.

When Jean Louise returned to Maycomb, Dill was one of the few people she first thought about. She was specially reminiscing memories with Dill at the time she faced the discoveries of Atticus and Maycomb's true nature.

Dill symbolizes a touchstone to Jean Louise's childhood, when everything was less complicated and she had a shield placed around her. Jean Louise only realized the changes, the loss of a friend, of what once was.

The Ice Cream Shop

Jean Louise visited the ice cream shop that was now built in their old home two times in the course of the novel. It was there that her some flashback memories came to her. This happened because she still sees the place as her home. The place symbolizes a 'before' state, where Jean Louise where everything is and what everything is.

When she discovered that Atticus has different convictions from her, she no longer found herself at home. Subconsciously, she visited her old neighborhood and home location, trying to get back to that place she called home.

Finch's Landing

Finch's Landing is a piece of land situated by a river that the Finch family owned. Jean Louise was surprised to learn that the property was sold despite. She understood the practicalities of selling the property and the family had no real use for the place. However, Finch Landing symbolized another touchstone to home for Jean Louise. When was learned of this transaction, she hadn't even found out about Atticus and Henry's participation in the Citizens' Council yet. Yet at that time, she entertained the idea of agreeing to marry Henry if he was able to give her Finch Landing back.

This signifies the small vestiges of inner struggle that Jean Louise was subconsciously experiencing when things around her were not as what she thought they would be.

Calpurnia

Calpurnia symbolizes the comforting and loving Mother figure in Jean Louise's life. She has known Jean Louise since she was very little and treated her like her own. Jean Louise respected and loved Calpurnia just as she would her real mother.

When Jean Louise visited Calpurnia in GSAW, she was hurt to find a detached Calpurnia and she knew right away that something was wrong.

Aunt Alexandra

Aunt Alexandra symbolizes another mother figure in Jean Louise's life. However, Aunt Alexandra was the always-disapproving Mother. Jean Louise respected her aunt; however, she just could not understand her way of thinking. Aunt Alexandra also signifies the kind of woman that Jean Louise is expected to be. No matter what she does and how she tries, Jean Louise couldn't really be that kind of person. Despite this, does not want to hurt her aunt either.

Atticus Finch

Atticus Finch symbolizes the seemingly-perfect father figure or role model. Jean Louise set him as her watchman. The one person who will tell her what is right and what is wrong. Obviously her world shatters when she finds out that he is racist and believes in completely the opposite things that he has showed Jean Louise.

This happens when we idealize people – when we fail to imagine people, even our beloved parents or role models, as complex persons and as persons who can make mistakes.

Plot Arguments

Jem's Death

One of the most surprising things in **Go Set a Watchman** is the mention of Jem's death. Jem was a beloved main character in To Kill a Mockingbird. This character death is not inevitable but it is understandable and well-justified in the book. However, for those who have grown up to love To Kill a Mockingbird, Jem's death can certainly be shocking. *Atticus is racist.*

This is another shocking revelation that Go Set a Watchman has brought. Atticus is a parable of human decency in Jean Louise's and TKAM reader's minds. When GSAW's story unfolds, readers are taken to a different understanding of Jean Louise's world. It is Jean Louise's reaction to such discovery that propels the story. How does one recover after being betrayed by your own father? Is that really a betrayal when you and your role model's convictions diverge?

Jean Louise and readers are taken to understand people like Atticus and somewhat see how their minds work.

Uncle Finch and how he was in love with Jean Louise' mother

Dr. Finch is dubbed the most learned licensed eccentric in Maycomb. His talk is always littered with Victorian literary quotes and phrases. This can be endearing. But when Jean Louise sought out her uncle for an explanation of Atticus' behavior, he went to this long and confusing narrative of personalities, their circumstances and famous words.

Jean Louise does not get the straight answer she wants. Reading chapters with him in it can be boring if one is not aware of the authors he is talking about. Jean Louise exasperation over this feeble man's blabbering was definitely called for.

Uncle Finch revealing his love for Jean Louise' mother explains his doting over her and Jem. Yet it keeps readers wondering how the love story really played out.

Childhood Flashbacks

Go Set a Watchman is filled with Jean Louise' childhood anecdotes in the form of flashbacks. This is an effective way of comparing and showing Jean Louise's life and mode thinking now and then. The funny snippets of Jean Louise's adolescence also feel consistent to the Scout that readers would know in TKAM. However, the flashbacks can be cumbersome and confusing to some readers who have not read TKAM or those not used to the story structure.

Tom Robinson Case Result Inconsistency

In TKAM, Tom Robinson was found guilty of the rape case and he died when he attempted to escape prison. However, in GSAW, Tom Robinson was acquitted of the crime. The rape case decision was one of the most pivoting moments in TKAM. When this plot point is changed in GSAW, it can affect how the book, and in effect Atticus, should be perceived. Was this an editorial mishap? Or a just a pre-edit draft of TKAM? This then lends credence to the belief that GSAW shouldn't have been published.

Publication Controversy

In February 2015, HarperCollins and the Harper Lee's estate announced that a sequel of To Kill a Mockingbird will be released after the rediscovery of its manuscript. Talks regarding whether the author was fully aware of this decision then emerged.

After all, Harper Lee is now in an assisted-living facility and is partially deaf and blind. All these news were subsequently shut down as concerned citizens and authorities living near Lee found that the author is fully aware and conscious of the publication decision.

This does not stop many individuals from wondering otherwise. It just seems so timely that just a few months after the author's sister (who was most protective of Harper Lee's work) died; the sequel manuscript was found and published.

Review Conclusion

Go Set a Watchman is an okay book as a sequel to To Kill a Mockingbird.

Go Set a Watchman is a great book in giving us a look into an author's writing process.

It couldn't be helped that GSAW will always be compared to TKAM. The two books now co-exist in the same world. Both their societal implications and themes are as applicable today.

GSAW is not as compelling as TKAM. It lacked the unique and naïve voice of young Scout which most people loved about TKAM. Even if we get glimpses of that in GSAW, the book was still told differently.

Perhaps there is a need for the storytelling to be different since Jean Louise is now older and the world is more different.

Jean Louise's specific path out of disillusionment as depicted in the book may be typical in real life but there was something to it that can make it feel disconnected and less relatable. However, the poignant message of discovering and being your own person is something that each of us should strive for in our life still rings true.

Nevertheless, let not this review be your watchman to the novel's merits; Go, set your own watchman and declare what you see.

Printed in Great Britain
by Amazon